To our dear friends
Gabe and Savannah

Jan. 2023

We love you and pray
The Lord's Blessing on your
beautiful family.

Hope you
enjoy our
family Story ... ♡

Tamara

D1518548

HOPE
HOUSE

Sanctuary

SAFE SPACES AND THE TRANSFORMING POWER OF THE HOME

Original Art and Text by

TAMARA GLASNER AND HER DAUGHTERS, JESSICA, EMILY, AND MADELINE

Editor: Jessica Glasner
Design: Jessica Glasner
Interior Artwork: Jessica Glasner and
Madeline Glasner-Bowman

Printed in the United States of
America

First Printing: 9798704720850
WWW.HOPEHOUSEPRESS.CO

So happy you came!

Jessica, thank you from the depths of my heart for your genius production of this little book. Emily, I am forever grateful for the encouragement you gave me to push through and finish. And Madi, thank you for the life and joy your art brought to these pages. You three are my favorite creative works. Finally, Lawrence, you are a prince of a man and the love of my life. I couldn't have done it without you.

Are You Ready to Build Your Sanctuary?

This book is a guide to making your home a safe haven for you, your family, and others. Consider it a family collage. My daughters contributed their artwork, poetry, and writings throughout and encouraged me to write our story. It is my prayer that you discover God's plan for your home to become a sanctuary.

With Love -Tamara

OUR QUEST TO MAKING OUR HOME A SANCTUARY STARTED OVER THIRTY YEARS AGO.

SANCTUARIES ARE SAFE SPACES.

PEACEFUL SPACES.

THEY ARE FAR MORE THAN FOUR WALLS AND A ROOF. SANCTUARIES LIVE INSIDE YOU AS MUCH AS YOU LIVE IN THEM.

SANCTUARIES OFFER PROTECTION. SANCTUARIES ARE SACRED. THEY ARE HOSPITABLE, HUMBLE, AND PRAYERFUL.

THEY ARE ARE FEARLESS AND FREE. THEY ARE BRIMMING OVER WITH HOPE. THEY GIVE ROOM FOR SOUL RESTORATION.

OUR SANCTUARY IS a place where Yeshua, JESUS, is welcome into every aspect of daily life.

HIS PRESENCE MAKES ALL THE DIFFERENCE, AND THAT IS WHY COMMUNION IS WHERE SANCTUARY BUILDING BEGINS.

"THEN LET THEM MAKE A SANCTUARY FOR ME AND I WILL DWELL AMONG THEM." -EXODUS 25:8

THE HOSPITABLE HOME

After Lawrence and I got married and began to make a home together in our first little condo, we started our adventures in hospitality. Lawrence and I truly wanted to have people in our home and felt that this was a part of God's plan for our marriage, knowing that the act of opening your home and letting people in is one of the most powerful ways of showing the love of the Father.

It took me a while, however, to get the hang of hosting. I was too worried about the house being perfect, the meal being perfect, the right music, the ambiance, what to wear, etc. - all things that are superficial at the end of the day. What's more, unfortunately, I was a nervous wreck before people came over. I got so uptight and edgy (i.e., upset at Larry for stupid reasons) that at one point my new husband said he didn't want to open the house anymore! The very thing God asked us to do was causing stress in our marriage and hindering the work of the Holy Spirit because, if you got right down to it, I had a control issue rooted in perfectionism. YIKES!

Thank goodness for His tender mercies! When we recognize where we've messed up and repent, He shows us a better way. For me, that means opening my home with a heart of love, not a heart of "perfect hostess."

No matter who is coming or how complicated it may seem, a heart of love will take care of almost every hard situation that comes through your door.

A HEART OF LOVE LOOKS LIKE:

PRAYING FOR THE EVENT BEFORE IT HAPPENS

HELPING EVERYONE FEEL ACCEPTED WITH
HUGS AND EYE-CONTACT

MAKING ROOM FOR WORSHIP AND SHARING
A WORD FROM THE WORD

MAKING ROOM TO PRAY FOR THOSE WHO
NEED PRAYER

NOT STICKING TOO CLOSELY TO YOUR
SCHEDULE

Family
Night

On Wednesday you're invited to our house. Every Wednesday. No need to RSVP. We'll be there.

Come around 6:00, bring a friend, we will gather around the table, holding hands and welcoming the Lord to be with us. We then will break the bread and pour the wine – and as we eat, and laugh, and tell stories – we'll heal in His presence.

We read scriptures, and sing worship with a guitar or two. Songs we all know, and songs no one knows because they are spur-of-the-moment, just inspired.

Sometimes we play games like Fishbowl or Ultimate Charades.

Often, there's a birthday to celebrate. Sometimes, a tear is shed and a weakness shared. In the safety of times together like our "Family Night," we discover we are not alone, and don't have to be.

There was a time when every Wednesday we could expect between 20 and 40 students to join us for dinner. My children remember this as one of the best seasons of their lives. Life-long friendships were built during that year, several marriages were born, and now, several of the internationals have carried family night back to Europe. The lesson is this: by keeping a regular schedule, friends knew they could join in for food, fun, and fellowship which created a foundation for real family to form.

RECIPE FOR FUN

WITHOUT HIS PRESENCE, THE NIGHT WOULD BE A COMPLETE LOSS. WHAT WE GIVE, IN TERMS OF PEACE, JOY, AND EVEN PHYSICAL GIFTS (LIKE FOOD AND THE ABILITY TO GIVE SOMEONE A HUG) ALL COME FROM HIM ANYWAYS! HE MAKES OUR HOME AND HEARTS FULL AND, OUT OF THE OVERFLOW, WE GIVE TO OTHERS. AS OUR PERSONAL SANCTUARIES ARE TRANSFORMED, WE HAVE ENDLESS LOVE TO GIVE AND RECEIVE.

AS A FAMILY, WE GATHER FOR A FEW MOMENTS TO PRAY AND INVITE THE HOLY SPIRIT TO BE PRESENT BEFORE EVERYONE ARRIVES. IF IT HAS BEEN A HARD OR TIRING DAY, WE ASK THE LORD TO HELP US FOCUS ON WHAT MATTERS AND GIVE US THE ENERGY WE NEED TO CREATE A SAFE PLACE FOR OUR GUESTS. HE HAS NEVER FAILED TO COME THROUGH. HE IS PRESENT AT EVERY GATHERING BECAUSE HE IS FAITHFUL. WE LET HIM FILL US SO WE CAN POUR OUT.

WE EMBRACE THE RULE OF "PERFECT PEACE, NOT PERFECTION." THE HOUSE IS CLEAN, DEFINITELY, BUT NOT SO CLEAN THAT PEOPLE FEEL NERVOUS ABOUT MESSING UP MY COUCH'S PILLOWS. DINNER IS SIMPLE AND EASY (AND NOT EXPENSIVE) TO PREPARE FOR A CROWD. I.E. WE DO A LOT OF PASTA AND BIG SALADS. FAMILY NIGHT IS NOT ABOUT IMPRESSING FOOD CRITICS. IT'S ABOUT FEEDING HEALTHY, SOUL NOURISHING FOOD TO HUNGRY PEOPLE. FINALLY, WE LET EVERYONE PITCH IN WHEN IT COMES TO CLEAN-UP TIME.

Emily's Poem

A door to hearts, open smiles.
With greetings and all places inside, away from storms.
There are those, together, bound, with love, can find joy.
AT THE TABLE.

A person of full heart, pure open heart.
With knocking, seeks to show the way through truth.
And in being, seeing, all-knowing, kneels to wash the feet.
In the home of those he loves.

There is time when who, if oneness bonds,
Takes the life of mortals to, through, till eternity.
And as newness settles forever as lasting dew,
Finds the joy of those who gather.

At last.

On the other side of the sun.

As it passes by, we find ourselves entwined in wholeness, in Him, as hope has become the tree fulfilled.

TOGETHER, AT THE TABLE.

Jesus opened up His table to us in communion and we now open our tables to each other for healing and wholeness.

SHARING YOUR LIVES AT THE TABLE MAKES WAY FOR DEEP AND LASTING FRIENDSHIPS ON THIS EARTH WHEN HONOR AND LOVE ARE INVITED. I BELIEVE THAT THE TABLE IS A PLACE WHERE WE CAN ALL BECOME A FAMILY, WHERE WE SHARE LAUGHTER AND TEARS ALONGSIDE BREAD AND WINE.

FRIENDSHIPS ARE FORMED AT THE TABLE. LOVE, TRUST, AND HOPE ARE FORGED... AT THE TABLE. TABLE TALK IS SACRED. WHERE ELSE CAN YOU COLLECTIVELY DISCUSS THE BIG QUESTIONS, DREAM CREATIVELY, AND PLAN FOR THE FUTURE? THERE IS NO LOCATION MORE CONDUCIVE TO GROWING CLOSER TO GOD AND EACH OTHER THAN THE TABLE.

I REMEMBER ONE SPECIAL GATHERING. THE CANDLES WERE LIT AND SOFT MUSIC PLAYED. A LOVELY COUPLE VISITING FROM OVERSEAS SHARED THEIR STORY OF A PERSONAL LOSS AND HOW TERRIBLY HARD IT HAD BEEN FOR THEM. LONG AFTER THAT NIGHT ENDED, WE LEARNED THAT THEY HAD NOT BEEN ASKED TO SHARE THEIR STORY BEFORE AND THAT EVENING HAD A DEEP IMPACT ON THEM. MAKING SPACE FOR OTHERS TO SHARE THEIR JOURNEY OPENS THE DOOR TO HEALING AND HOPE FOR THE FUTURE IN A WAY ONLY COMMUNION WITH THE BODY OF CHRIST CAN.

DO ASK PEOPLE HOW THEY ARE AND GIVE
THEM ROOM TO BE HEARD AND SHARE
THEIR STORY.

DON'T TALK ABOUT DIVISIVE SUBJECTS.
THOSE CONVERSATIONS CAN BE HELD
LATER. REMEMBER: THE TABLE IS A SAFE
SPACE FOR EVERYONE.

Embrace Celebration

Our family loves to celebrate. Birthday breakfasts. Every holiday. Every victory, no matter how small. Because of Larry's Jewish heritage, we embrace the Jewish festivals as well (Jesus did too!). Every Friday is sacred because it is the beginning of Shabbat. Every Friday, we break the bread and drink the wine, we welcome in the Shabbat with songs that Jesus sang, and we enter into the divine rest ordained when God finished creating the world.

As a side note, we keep things simple. If something is too complicated or too intense, it sucks the joy out of what God intended to be a life-giving recharge. The joy of celebrating is keeping things simple enough that you are not overwhelmed in the process of preparing to celebrate. It also makes it much easier on your guests if they know you were not stressed out preparing for their visit.

Let your speech always be gracious, seasoned with salt, so that you may know how you ought to answer each person.

Colossians 4:6

Come in,

Let's sing and dance together a song of thanksgiving.

Let us worship together the Lord our God.

And when you leave, remember that what went on within these walls was a small reflection of heaven,

A small taste of the family of God.

"FOR I KNOW THE PLANS I HAVE FOR YOU," DECLARES THE LORD, "PLANS TO PROSPER YOU AND NOT TO HARM YOU, PLANS TO GIVE YOU HOPE AND A FUTURE." ~JEREMIAH 29:11

I have a hope.

Hope for my family

Hope for healing

Hope for love

Hope for joy

Hope for life

Hope for safety

Hope for restoration

WE HAVE A HOPE.

FOR IN THIS HOPE WE WERE SAVED;
BUT HOPE THAT IS SEEN IS NO HOPE AT
ALL. WHO HOPES FOR WHAT HE CAN
ALREADY SEE? ~ ROMANS 8:24

LOVE STORY

How the Lord puts people together is one of the great mysteries. We all have dreams of our lives and what we hope for. Mine was to marry a man after the heart of God. I wanted to serve God first and truly didn't want a marriage built on any other foundation. So even at a young age I was praying for the right match. Prayer! Prayer is such a beautiful gift to us. We can connect to God each and every hour of the day with all of our heart's thoughts. We can listen to him in return. Prayer! I love little prayers. Nothing is too small for him to listen to. Nothing is too big either.

I met Lawrence at a wedding in Houston, Texas when I was still in junior high. I overheard him talking to friends about his journey to faith in which he had met Jesus the year before. He was alive with LOVE for Jesus. His words pointed to a man whose heart was on fire. What a journey he'd been on! It was wild, crazy, and filled with the touches of a God whose love goes to the end of the earth to find the lost sheep.

That's when I prayed this little prayer, "Lord, I would like to marry a man like Lawrence one day." For me, I thought I was letting the Lord know I wanted to marry a man after God's heart. I knew I didn't want anything less.

It was just a little prayer. But the Lord hears little prayers. In fact, my life is made up of lots of little prayers. (So be careful what you pray for!)

Now, did I think the answer to my prayer would actually be Lawrence? I'm not sure. He was an adult, and I was just a little junior high schooler. Lawrence was definitely a terrific role model and perhaps a standard to aim for.

After my cousin's wedding ended, our family went back home and I went back to junior high school where I told my best friend, Dori, about the wedding and how I met this guy, Lawrence. (Dori was such a good friend. She didn't laugh at me, but rather, she listened to me and made me feel it was a valuable dream.)

Well, the years went by and life was moving on. I kept Lawrence in the back of mind as my standard and didn't want anyone less than him - in character, drive, passion, or spirit.

Meanwhile, Lawrence didn't even remember meeting me at that wedding. Remember, I was just a young girl. I thought he would be married long before I grew up. But God kept him single, just for me.

Little Prayers, Big Answers: A Honeymoon Story

Something really wonderful happened when I was a sophomore in high school.

My father, who was an award winning architect in Texas, was invited to go to Dallas to view a remodeled mansion that had been converted into a gorgeous boutique hotel, The Mansion at Turtle Creek. This was what my family did for fun: we visited beautiful houses all over the country and Europe to study the architecture both new and old. (It's a love that's continued through the years.)

The Mansion at Turtle Creek had not yet officially opened to the public. Only certain architects and designers were allowed on the tour. From the moment we pulled up, I knew this was a very special hotel. First of all, the grounds were covered with huge trees, and azaleas, a beautiful fountain in the middle of the drive next to the main entrance. The lobby had tall ceilings with gorgeous windows that could have been in Versailles. Wood floors and marble tables covered with gloriously tall floral arrangements were everywhere you looked. All the colors were natural and soft. I loved it.

Our guide led us from the lobby to the sophisticated wood-paneled intimate dining room that had once served as the mansion's library. This hotel was going to be a popular hotel in Dallas, hosting global dignitaries and celebrities. Even when the mansion was privately owned, the guest list was impressive. President Franklin D. Roosevelt and Tennessee Williams were regulars.

As we were led through the different rooms, the last stop was the main suite on the upper floor.

This suite was perfectly orchestrated. French doors, marble bathrooms, and linens and colors that were truly palace-like. It was the largest, most lovely suite in the hotel with three rooms and a balcony looking out over the garden. The bed was surrounded by floor to ceiling curtains with large European-style comforters and pillows with the finest cotton sheets. It was romance defined.

The tour went into the enormous bathroom. A huge oval marble tub and matching walk-in marble shower. Marble floors! The most beautiful marble you have ever seen. The attention to detail and perfection was breathtaking.

When everyone left the bathroom, I hung back a few seconds. I had to take it in by myself. Without even really thinking about what I was doing, I put my hands on the wall next to the sink and the door and said, "Lord, if there is any way, I would love to stay here on my honeymoon."

I KNOW! Kind of a crazy little prayer for a high school sophomore... But you had to see that bathroom to understand what I was feeling. Again, another LITTLE prayer rolling out of my mouth.

I am a firm believer that God loves it when we dream. We may not see every prayer we pray answered, but that is not always the point. Being open about our dreams with our Heavenly Father builds intimacy and joy. As long as we do not try to control Him and the outcome, and truly believe He knows what is best for us, we will grow closer and closer to Him as we live day to day.

No one even noticed I was not with the group for those few moments, and I kept this little prayer a secret, just between me and the Lord.

Fast-forward several years to the summer after my high school graduation. I'm working at a camp as a counselor teaching water skiing and tennis for the summer months until it was time to head off to college in September. The camp was close enough for me to drive home every other weekend so I could see my family.

On one of these weekends home, I met up with a few friends at a pizza place in town. My sister ended up joining us with the express purpose to let me know that there was a, "very special guest" visiting our family who would be speaking at our church the next evening and I should make plans to go hear him.

I decided I would go and hear whoever this "mystery" guest was. Lo and behold, it was none other than Lawrence Glasner. Remember him? I had prayed I could marry someone like him when I was 12. And here he was, STILL very single.

He was sitting with my parents in the front row of the church preparing to share the story of how he, a Jewish guy from New York, came to meet his Messiah. I was sitting on the back row of the church because I had to leave early to get back to the camp.

But you better believe me when I made sure I got the next weekend off and drove back home where I'd learned Lawrence was staying with my family for the weekend.

When I arrived at home, I looked at him, he looked at me. I was no longer a little girl. And here, in my own home, was this guy I had prayed for so long ago! What was God doing? Needless to say, we were soon engaged.

As we got close to the wedding date, we began to plan our honeymoon and, in the process, I remembered that wonderful hotel we had visited when I was in high school. The one that I prayed to spend my honeymoon in while I paused in the marble bathroom on the tour.

"Let's try to stay there a night before we go to Hawaii," I said.

Larry, sweet as always, told me he would check into it.

"Well," he said after he checked into it, "We can stay in that suite for a night or go to Hawaii for two weeks. Price is the same."

"Hawaii." I said, inwardly laughing that it was so expensive.

"But I was able to get one of the smaller rooms that was in our budget. Maybe not quite as ritzy, but it will still be fun."

Our wedding was beautiful, an outdoor ceremony held under enormous old oaks and willows. Music, always an important part of our lives, was an integral aspect of the program, with a small classical ensemble and wonderful acoustic worship. Surrounded by our family and friends, we said "I do," and were off and running as a married couple.

I'll never forget getting out of the taxi and entering the lobby of the Mansion. I was wearing my cute little red "going away" suit, with a matching hat. Lawrence and I were so excited for our honeymoon. Like any young bride, I sat on one of those gilded couches and waited for Larry to check us in.

I couldn't hear exactly what was going on at the front desk, but it quickly became clear that there was some sort of mix-up. Larry turned back and looked at me with an expression that made my heart sink. He walked back to where I sat. "Tammy, the hotel has no record of our reservation."

"What?"

"No record!" He inhaled, "Not only that, the desk guy told me that there is a business conference going on right now and every room in the hotel is occupied."

Lawrence had told the clerk that he had made these reservations weeks ago. It was his honeymoon. The clerk felt awful for him "He said he was going to go talk to the manager."

After what seemed like an eternity, the clerk returned with the manager and looked at us.

"Well, we do have ONE room left in the hotel, and I think you will like it. And we will let you have this room for the same rate as the regular rooms."

Larry and I looked at one another and shrugged as the bell hop came and got our luggage. As we got on a tiny elevator, I was suspicious. It felt familiar.

When we got out, there was The Suite! The one I had prayed for years before, the one where I put my hands on the wall of the bathroom asking my Father God for this blessing for this specific moment. At the time, I can honestly say I did not realize the power of little prayers. But trust me, little prayers have big power.

A monumental avalanche of God's love came barreling down on my heart and I began to cry. He said yes to this little desire and dream of mine and caused every date to collide so Larry and I could stay there.

Of course, I have prayed scores of prayers that the Lord so graciously DID NOT answer, because He knows those prayers would not have been the best for me. But... on many occasions I remind myself of the honeymoon miracle, because while He does not say yes to every prayer, occasionally, He does give us the desires of our hearts.

The Greatest Romance

How amazing is the Lord's love for us! This is the greatest romance of all! The romance with the King of Kings, and the Lord of Lords.

YES, He is the great romance of our lives. His love never dies. His love never fails. His love is constant and sure. He never says He is done. He never ever walks out or says He is finished with us. He is forever our dearest, most trusted friend. The Bible says He will NEVER leave us or forsake us.

NEVER. Through eternity.

No one can ever replace this love. NO ONE. Do you hear me? He is forever the closest love of your life.

He said in Psalm 37:4, "Delight yourself in the Lord, and He will give you your heart's desire."

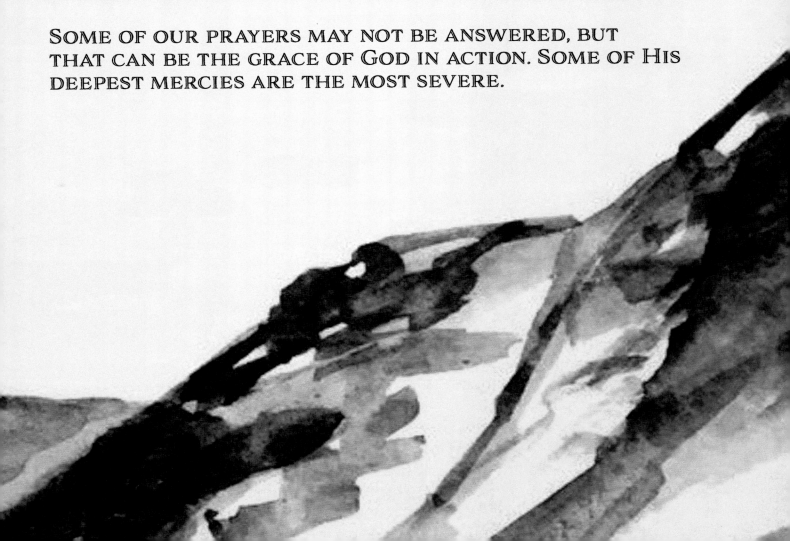

This is Good News! First, we delight ourselves in the Lord. Then, His desires will become ours.

If our one desire is to be with the Lord, our lives will be filled with Him and filled with His beauty.

Some of our prayers may not be answered, but that can be the grace of God in action. Some of His deepest mercies are the most severe.

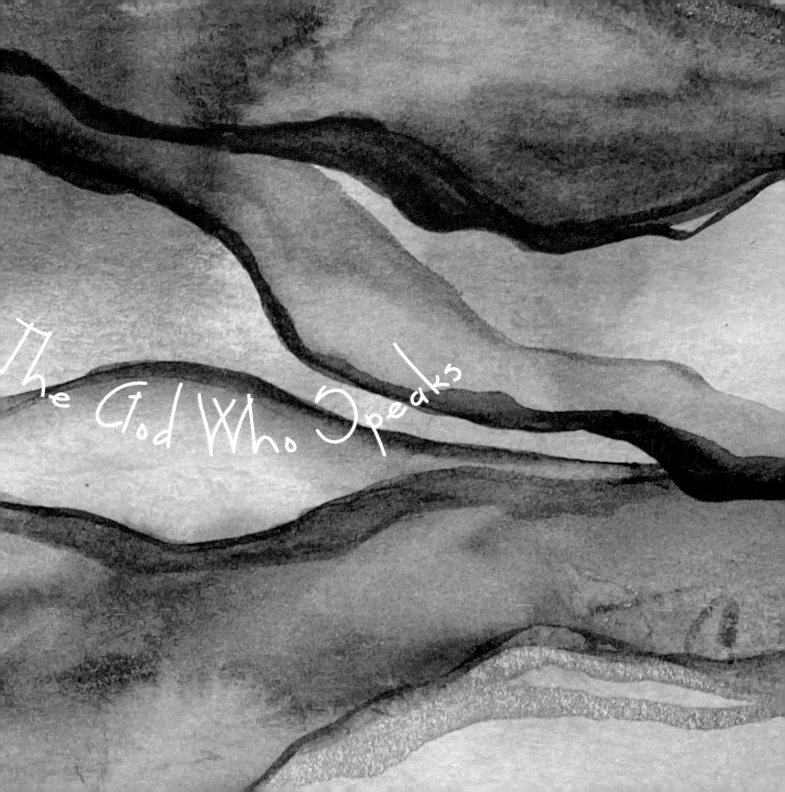

The Still Small Voice

The Lord has a way of growing and maturing us to do the right thing and teaching us how to live, and how to forgive and to love people even when they are ugly to us. Oftentimes, these lessons begin in childhood. I know that every time we stop ourselves from that first bad response and quietly go to God and listen to what he would tell us to do... we somehow are winning a battle.

Listening to that still small voice requires one to be quiet and still in the midst of the problem, the whirlwind, and the torment, and trust He will work all things out for your good. Sometimes, in the heat of the moment, it is difficult to listen, but those are the times when it is most important. I remember when my family moved from the great big Houston metropolis to a tiny Texas town built on the side of a lake.

I was the new girl in town.

Seventh grade. (Gulp.)

Gym class was over and I was in the girls' locker room changing back into my clothes for the next period. I was almost ready when two girls began to make a racket about someone stealing their lunch money. It was a little unnerving the way they were going on, and as I put on my right boot, I could feel some loose change with my toes. It hit me like a load of bricks. Oh man... these girls were trying to set me up! I could feel a knot of panic form in the pit of my stomach. That was my signal to pray.

"Lord, what do I do? No one knows me here. No one knows what kind of person I am. It will look like I stole their money. What should I do?"

Immediately I heard the voice of the Holy Spirit. "Tamara, pretend you don't feel the money down in your shoe. You did not put it there, so you don't know it is there."

"Alright Lord."

I proceeded to put the other boot on, grabbed my back-pack, and left the locker room (praying!).

As I walked through the gym to leave, these two girls started calling to me to stop.

"What do you guys want?" I asked. I had a kind of boldness. "I have to hurry to my next class, I don't want to be late."

Awkwardly, they began to explain that they needed to talk to me about this little prank they had played on me and how they had put the money down in my boot. Just like that, they came clean. I started to take off the wrong boot (on purpose) so that they would have to speak out that they knew just where it was. Lo and behold, they did. I took off that boot and poured their money into their hands. Filled with awe at how the Lord had protected me and exposed these girls' sin, I looked them in the eye and said strongly, "Don't ever do that again!"

I cannot help but wonder what would have happened if I had not listened to the voice of the Holy Spirit that first moment in the locker room when I slipped my foot into my boot.

I wish I could say that I always stop and listen the way I did in that locker room. There are many instances when I forget and move to action with my own bright ideas. (The results are never stellar.) But, when I do remember and respond with God's help, what a difference for me and all those around me.

In my opinion, one of the most important ways we can serve the Lord is to listen, trust, and obey. Simple acts like walking out of a room, going to check on a neighbor, saying the right words, or staying quiet, can save relationships, lead people to Jesus, and unlock opportunities for restoration. Thankfully, God is gracious and when we mess up or don't stop to listen, He always gives us another chance!

SANCTUARIES ARE HOUSES OF PRAYER. DISCIPLINE YOURSELF TO LISTEN TO GOD DAILY AND PUT INTO PRACTICE WHAT HE SAYS. REMEMBER: PRAYER IS THE KEY TO HOPE, AND HOPE OPENS THE DOOR TO JOY.

Daily read the Word. God's voice will always align with His written Word, so in order to know what He is saying to you in the moment, you need to know what He's already spoken through the Bible.

Daily cast your cares. It's difficult to hear God's voice if you are bogged down by fear and worry. Trust God to help you through whatever you face, every day.

Daily wait on the Lord. Give Him time and space to speak to you. Go on a walk. Arrange a prayer corner or prayer closet. Spend several minutes in worship, singing along with a recording or by yourself.

Daily step out. When you hear God's voice, don't hesitate to act on what He is saying. If He is encouraging you to be more loving with others, start loving NOW. If He whispers to call a friend to check in, do it immediately. Step out and practice what He teaches. You don't have to get it right every time, but the Lord rewards those who obey Him.

When you make your home a sanctuary, it becomes a safe place for others to become whole and strong and filled with purpose and joy.

EVERY FAMILY IS UNIQUE.

WHAT MAKES US LAUGH MAY NOT MAKE YOU LAUGH. WHAT WE FIGHT OVER MAY NOT BE WHAT YOU FIGHT OVER. WHAT WE VALUE MAY BE DIFFERENT. GOD LOVES DIFFERENCES. HE LOVES THAT EVERY PERSON AND EVERY FAMILY IS SPECIAL. GOD DOESN'T WANT A BUNCH OF COOKIE-CUTTER FAMILIES WHO ALL LOOK THE SAME. THAT IS WHY IT IS SO IMPORTANT THAT YOU MAKE YOUR HOME AND FAMILY JUST RIGHT FOR YOU, FILLED WITH TIMES AND MEMORIES THAT NO ONE ELSE WILL OR CAN EVER HAVE.

BUT, IN THE KINGDOM, SOME THINGS ARE UNIVERSAL. EVERY HEALTHY, CLOSE FAMILY IS BUILT ON LOVE. AND A HOME FILLED WITH LOVE IS A SANCTUARY.

HOW DO YOU BUILD A FOUNDATION OF LOVE? ROMANS 12:9-21 (NIRV) LAYS IT OUT STEP BY STEP.

"Love must be honest and true. HATE what is EVIL. Hold on to what is good."

"Love each other deeply. Honor others more than yourselves."

"Never let the fire in your heart go out. Keep it alive. Serve the Lord."

"When you hope, be joyful. When you suffer, be patient. When you pray, be faithful."

"Share with God's people who are in need. Welcome others into your homes."

"Bless those who hurt you. Bless them, and do not call down curses on them."

"Be joyful with those who are joyful. Be sad with those who are sad."

"Agree with each other. Don't be proud."

"Be willing to be a friend of people who aren't considered important."

"Don't think that you are better than others."

When our girls were young, we helped them memorize Romans 12:9–21 so their foundations would be strong and secure for future relationships.

vs 9: "Love must be honest and true. HATE what is EVIL. Hold on to what is good."

In a culture that often embraces what is evil and loves lies, this verse can be difficult to apply. But it can be done. Talk openly with your family about what is true and honest. Discipline yourselves to talk and think about what is lovely. As a parent, don't hesitate to explain why we must hate evil. What you consume (read, watch, listen to, etc.) is a great thermometer on whether you hate evil, tolerate it, or even welcome it because it is "popular" or "just a _____" (fill in the blank). An open door to evil, no matter how subtle, is an open door to the deceiver. And deception of any kind is one of the first things that can crack a family's firm foundation.

vs. 10: "Love each other deeply. Honor others more than yourselves."

This one speaks for itself. Love your family without hesitation or conditions. Put their needs above your own. Treat your children and spouse with respect. Listen to them and value their opinions, dreams, and goals (and do what you can to help them reach them). When a whole family embraces this verse, and each member consistently honors and loves, a miraculous bond forms called *true community*.

vs. 11: "Never let the fire in your heart go out. Keep it alive. Serve the Lord."

The importance of family worship and devotions can't be overstated. Don't leave your family's spiritual health to a once-a-week service. Pray together daily, read scripture individually and together regularly, and sing praise songs throughout the week. We often pull out the guitar and sing a song or two after dinner. I love keeping scripture songs or my favorite worship albums playing through the house as I go about my day, and some seasons through the night (quietly).

vs. 12: "When you hope, be joyful. When you suffer, be patient. When you pray, be faithful."

When you have been married over thirty years, watched your husband go in and out of the hospital more times than you can count, spent many sleepless nights in the ICU, watched your children reach for the stars and occasionally crash land when they come back down, had your heart broken by those you trusted more than you knew was possible, you will know that sometimes it is hard to stay joyful, patient, or faithful. And yet, this is exactly what God commands us to do. When we call out for His help in times of trouble, when you don't get the job or into the school of choice, when sickness lingers, when God seems to be waiting until eternity to answer your prayers, He will give us what we need to go another day.

Sometimes, it is a day-by-day (even a minute-by-minute!) battle to hold on to joy, patience, and faith, but it is well worth the fight. Close families are the ones that can weather the storm together in quiet expectation that help is on the way and the realization that God knows exactly what He is doing, even if we don't understand.

vs. 13: "Share with God's people who are in need. Welcome others into your homes."

Life is better together. As a family, one of our core values is to maintain an open home. There is rarely a time when the guest room is not full. And if it is, we have a comfortable couch! Now, I want to be clear: this verse does not say "share when you have extra" or "welcome others when you feel like it." In order to really embrace this command, your family will need a collective agreement to give to others in times of lack, pain, and sheer tiredness.

When my husband was scheduled for open heart surgery several years ago, my daughters (who were at home) hosted a prayer party. They made dinner for their friends and celebrated together what they trusted God would do: heal and protect their father through the seven hour procedure.

At a time when they were in emotional need, they gave. The result? A night that could have been one of the most stressful of their lives was filled with joy and peace and worship. Welcoming and sharing what you have with others can actually be the key to bringing your family together.

Having a few extra people around can help hold attitudes in check, teach your children how to get along with others and be faithful friends in good times and bad, and keeps your family honest and open. Why? Because when you share what you have, it opens the door to letting other people share your burdens in a tangible, profound way.

vs. 14: "Bless those who hurt you. Bless them, and do not call down curses on them."

I think everyone knows that it can be difficult to bless those who curse you. When a child is unkind, when people you trust betray you, or when strangers are outright rude, don't give them the same treatment.

As a family, practice blessing, not cursing. Teach your children to repay evil with good (where better to learn this than with siblings!) and model this behavior with your spouse.

vs. 15: "Be joyful with those who are joyful. Be sad with those who are sad."

There is an old saying that no mother is happier than her saddest child. It's important to be sensitive to the emotional needs of your family. Let your children cry and comfort them. Be a safe place for your spouse to share their heart. At the same time, this verse warns us not to be killjoys. We welcome laughter and fun! Goodness knows that life is hard enough as it is. When joy comes, revel in it. Lawrence and I sometimes have to put on extra patience to let the good times roll!

Sometimes, my girls get laughing so hard and loud I worry what the neighbors will think! But... what can I say, happiness is a gift from the Lord. I prayed laughter would fill our house, and it has!

vs. 16: "Agree with each other. Don't be proud."

Lawrence, my husband, is a lawyer, and a good one. He is a fighter for justice. This is awesome, but by nature, he's argumentative... a family trait that surfaces in our children on occasion. It's taken us a long time to learn how to keep our mouths shut and not argue the finer points of (*you fill in the blank*). Maintaining a position over stupid issues (like whether or not Cousin Joe will be admiral in five years or seven) is another way to say, "this is how to ruin dinner, the day, or the week." It's also a way to lose your children's respect, while at the same time modeling behavior you don't want them to emulate. Pride destroys relationships, and petty arguments destroy peace. That's not to say some things aren't worth arguing over. Moral issues, ungodly behavior, etc., need to be combated (in love).

Remember, iron sharpens iron! But pride (the ungodly kind) is a strong enemy that should not be allowed in your home. Being humble and servant-hearted goes a long way to making your home amazing!!!

vs. 16: "Be willing to be a friend of people who aren't considered important."

The truth is, at some point, we've all been impressed with people because of their résumé, their level of influence, talent, fame, or the crowd they run with. Then, on closer inspection, we are faced with the hard reality that their character doesn't line up with their message. Perhaps they aren't kind to the "little people," or maybe they are shallower than their image on social media reflects.

I know this sounds basic, but everyone needs to be reminded - no matter what - not to choose their community based on social status, ethnicity, or culture. It is a big mistake to seek out friends because you want to be a part of their clique or you want to be regarded as powerful, popular, or whatever it is they have that you want through association. Choose your friends (and help your children choose friends) based on the answer to one simple question: Are they a good friend?

A good friend is one who comes through, allows you to be your authentic self, pulls you up when your down, and is trustworthy. A good friend is in it for what they can give, not what they can get. If you study friendship in the Bible, it becomes pretty clear that friendship has nothing to do with whether or not someone is important. That's not to say your friends may not be important or famous people! They may be – but that should not be the reason you are friends.

This verse has profound implications for society. When you treat all people, no matter what their job is, with equal generosity, care, and hospitality, you are stepping into the shoes of Jesus. You are stopping racism, prejudice, and bigotry right where it starts – at home. By making your home a sanctuary for everyone, regardless of position, you are doing your part to demonstrate the true nature of what it means to be a part of the family of God.

We've hosted some important people in our years of opening our home. Some were very important, diplomatic delegations from the Middle East, Bishops from Africa, and world-famous athletes. It's an amazing thing, but when you sit around a table eating a meal, titles tend to disappear. People become people. If you keep this in mind, no matter who you are hosting, you will steer clear of falling into the trap of respecting someone or seeking their friendship based on the wrong things. Remember too that important people were, at one time in their lives, not important. And they will remember how you treated them when they were a (*fill in the blank* that you consider menial). The teenager bagging your groceries might one day be the president. Do you really want to be the one person who stands out in his memory as a great big snob?

vs. 16: "Don't think that you are better than others."

Is there really more to say about this one? No. I don't think so. Paul said it all when he said, "Don't think you are better than others." You are not. Your family is not. We all have our stuff and at the end of the day, we all stand before God alone. We would do well to remember this daily. It keeps pride from settling in and hardening our hearts to correction and growth.

Sometimes, as believers, it is easy to think we are doing better than other people. We aren't going around "sinning" (maybe!), we are checking off the right boxes, etc. The thing is, we are held to a different standard than those who don't know Jesus. We all have areas of our lives we need to resubmit to Jesus, sometimes daily. Whether it is anger, bitterness, lust, greed, jealousy, pride, or what-have-you, get real about where your heart is.

We all need Jesus more than ever, and the more you know Him,
the more you know you need Him.

The most important job of a believer in creating a sanctuary is to guard your gates.

There are many gates in life. The eye-gate. The thought-gate. The desire-gate. The influence-gate. We are all gatekeepers. Mothers and fathers are gatekeepers of their families. Adults are gatekeepers of their own hearts and spirits. We each have individual and communal gates to keep, as we each care for individuals (where we live inside our hearts and minds) and communal sanctuaries (where we live with others, our homes, churches, schools, etc.). Protecting the sanctity and peace of these sanctuaries, the inside ones and the outside ones, is the foundation for preventing anxiety, stress, worry, and discord.

The gatekeeper allows certain things inside the sanctuary and keeps other things out.

The gatekeeper knows who is allowed inside (peace, patience, kindness, truth, the things that matter and make us better) and the gatekeeper also knows what is not allowed inside (striving, petty arguments, meanness, and influences that encourage us to think and act like the world). The gatekeeper has the gift of discernment to know right from wrong, good from evil, and friend from foe. They daily ask God to give them wisdom. With the help of heaven, the gatekeepers protect the sanctity of the home. They aren't afraid to say "no," turn off the TV when necessary, change music, switch to a different game or address destructive behavior (you get the idea). They are quick to welcome joy and laughter. And the boundaries they set around their garden protects the innocence and integrity of the young plants growing. The gatekeeper vigilantly seeks peace, sometimes putting up quite a fight to achieve it!

Let me make it clear, gatekeeping is not legalism. Gatekeeping is STEWARDSHIP. One does not guard the gate to get good marks or look a certain way. One guards the gate because what is inside is so precious and irreplaceable that it must be protected from thieves, robbers, and those who would destroy growing things before they reach maturity.

THE KEY TO EFFECTIVE GATEKEEPING IS SIMPLE PRAYER....

WHEN LAWRENCE AND I WERE ENGAGED, WE HAD THE CONVERSATION ABOUT RAISING OUR KIDS. YOU KNOW, THAT CONVERSATION WHICH IS COMPLETELY MYSTERIOUS WHEN YOU'VE NEVER HAD CHILDREN. THE CONVERSATION THAT TRIES TO HELP CLARIFY HOW YOU WILL LIVE AS PARENTS AND PARTNERS, ETC. WE DECIDED THAT WE WOULD RELENTLESSLY PROTECT OUR CHILDREN'S CREATIVITY.

NOW, LET ME GET SOMETHING STRAIGHT RIGHT NOW: THERE IS NO PERFECT GATEKEEPER ON EARTH. NO PERFECT PARENT. NO PERFECT KID. THERE JUST ISN'T. WE ARE ALL ON A JOURNEY. EVERYONE MAKES MISTAKES AND EACH ONE OF US WILL FACE HARDSHIPS IN LIFE BECAUSE OF THE MISTAKES WE MAKE. WE ALL NEED THE WONDERFUL LOVING TOUCH OF GOD TO HEAL THE BROKENNESS THAT COMES ALONG THE WAY. I HAVE MADE SO MANY ERRORS IN PARENTING! IN BEING A LOVING WIFE! IN BEING A GRACIOUS FRIEND! BUT WITH THE HELP OF JESUS, WE LIVE IN FORGIVENESS AND SEE HIS AMAZING PROTECTION OVER OUR RELATIONSHIPS. BECAUSE OF THE COMMITMENT LAWRENCE AND I MADE SO MANY YEARS AGO TO PROTECT OUR CHILDREN'S CREATIVITY AND FOSTER THEIR GROWTH, THEY ARE EACH STILL ACTIVELY ENGAGED IN THE ARTS. THEY WATCHED LAWRENCE AND I VIGILANTLY GUARD THE GATES, AND THEY UNDERSTOOD HOW IMPORTANT IT IS FOR THEM TO FOLLOW SUIT.

As I joined hands with Lawrence, my husband, in holy matrimony, our journey as keepers of the sanctity of the home began. That meant when we identified an intruder, we would go after it until it was removed and our sanctuary was secure again. Attitudes, bad habits that hurt us or others, unhealthy forms of communication, things we went to to satisfy us other than the Lord, and many other enemies have been identified over the years, knocking at our gate under the guise of "it's easier to say nothing than talk about it," "we've always done it this way," and "but everyone else likes it or does it this way." These disguised enemies are often joined with the lie that peace comes through them. They are decoys of truth. Any peace they offer is a false peace. These decoys will do more damage than good. The messes they make can take years to clean up.

God supplies His gatekeepers with wisdom from His Spirit, His Word, and His people. Lawrence and I have found much-needed solutions to parenting and marriage questions through His Word, books, counselors, spiritual retreats, and trusted friends. Sometimes God speaks to us directly about an issue with solutions we never could have come up with on our own. He teaches us how to fight whatever battle we are fighting. We've learned over thirty years together that if we keep trying and do not give up, we will win, because He has already won.

THE HIDING PLACE

A sanctuary is a place of refuge, a haven, a safe harbor. It is a place void of the darkness and distraction of the world outside. A place where one can breathe and rest. In such a sanctuary, life has the ability to thrive. A sanctuary-home becomes a place where one is unashamed to sing or dance or create, without FEAR of rejection. It is a safe harbor, where all that is good and worthy is welcome, a refuge for family, friends and strangers.

You are my hiding place; You preserve me from trouble; You surround me with songs of deliverance.

Psalm 32:7

The process of making a home a sanctuary begins in the heart. Out of the overflow of making our heart a sanctuary for God comes the ability to make our homes a dwelling place for others to experience the love and safety only He can provide. When a family sets its heart on making their home a sanctuary for others, miracles happen. Hearts are healed. Spirits are nourished. And the truth of God's love is given space to penetrate the lie our culture spreads that life is meant to be spent independently fulfilling our selfish desires.

However, I've learned through experience that the peaceful sanctuary does not just happen; it must be fought for. As we live each day, the decisions we make impact those living in our home. When the peace gets rattled, we go to God for solutions to restore our home's shalom. We've discovered the vital importance of letting God into the mundane decisions of everyday life.

But first and foremost, we've embraced the invaluable truth that welcoming people into our lives and homes is a genuine reflection of how Jesus opened the door to welcome us into His family.

Our Family Song

LORD PREPARE ME, TO BE A SANCTUARY

PURE AND HOLY, TRIED AND TRUE

WITH THANKSGIVING

I'LL BE A LIVING, SANCTUARY

FOR YOU

~RANDY ROTHWELL

WE WANT TO BE A LIVING SANCTUARY FOR GOD: HOLY, TRIED AND TRUE, AND LIVING IN THANKSGIVING.

BECOMING A SANCTUARY IS A JOURNEY. IT TAKES TIME. IT MEANS NOT RUNNING AWAY FROM PAINFUL MOMENTS THAT MIGHT KEEP US FROM BECOMING SANCTUARIES.

NEXT TIME YOU HAVE A HUGE MISUNDERSTANDING OR ARGUMENT WITH ONE OF YOUR FAMILY MEMBERS, GO LOW AND SLOW, AND IN YOUR MIND PRAY FOR THE LORD TO GIVE YOU EARS TO HEAR AND JUST THE RIGHT WORDS TO BRING ABOUT UNDERSTANDING AND TRUTH. ASK HIM, "WHAT DO I SAY NOW? WHAT WILL SOFTEN THIS MOMENT?"

DON'T RUN FROM THE MOMENT.

DON'T IGNORE THE MOMENT.

FACE THE MOMENT HEAD-ON.

CHOOSE THE BETTER WAY. BE RELENTLESS! DON'T THROW IN THE TOWEL NO MATTER HOW MUCH YOU WANT TO. IT WILL PASS! I TELL YOU, THE LORD CAN MAKE A TERRIBLE AWFUL MOMENT SOFT AGAIN WITH HIS HELP. HE BRINGS HUMBLE HEARTS BACK TOGETHER EVERY TIME.

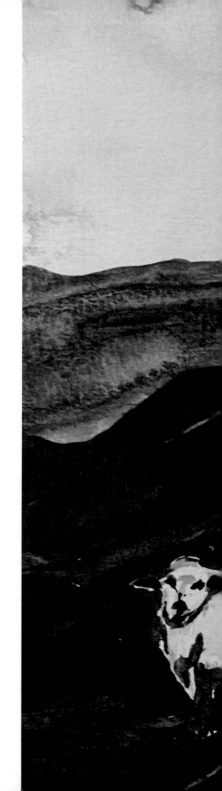

The Humble Home

Raising children is a privilege and a joy.

It is also, perhaps, the most difficult, high-risk thing anyone can attempt to do. The responsibility of keeping a child alive, healthy, and happy is enormous. The responsibility of helping a child reach their full potential brings up the pressure a notch or two. And then there is the responsibility of fostering a child's understanding of and relationship with God! It is incredible to me that God trusts us with children!

Lawrence and I worked hard to help our children learn the art of friendship at early ages. We refused to allow them to remain bitter or unforgiving towards one another. Remember, children at young ages are soft, pliable and teachable. You can help your children love well while they are learning to get along with their siblings. Relational skills learned at four will carry them through their whole lives.

A constant stream of guests came through our house, some for a night or two, some for months at a time. The girls watched and learned as Lawrence and I served, hosted, prayed for, and loved people of all ages and backgrounds. From foreign diplomats to plumbers and carpenters working on the house, they never knew who would be staying for dinner. But they knew whoever was at the table was there to be blessed, and so, as they grew, they joined in the ministry time, helping me prepare the house and the meals, praying together, and helping Lawrence lead worship. There were many powerful testimonies that emerged from these golden years. Jesus healed people from drug addictions and touched broken marriages. Others were declared cancer-free, while some were filled with hope after having lost everything.

God wanted us to value every single person who entered our home, no matter what. The Lord wanted every single person to feel they were home, even if it was only for a few hours a week.

You cannot have sweet romance when you are offended.

I don't remember what the argument was about, but I do remember how Lawrence was so frustrated with me (and I with him). It was very early in our marriage, and I ran out the door and drove away to a place I could cry and pray and call out to the Lord for help. (This was a time the Lord was speaking to both of us about our pride and strong wills.) I remember feeling so sad with no idea what to do next. The Lord spoke to me a word I will never forget and still remind myself of daily. The key to your marriage is humility.

Humility. What a powerful word.

There was a moment when both Lawrence and I realized that we could quickly demolish our beautiful love with selfish and unproductive misunderstandings and arguments. It was a scary, very real moment. We both had to learn how to disagree. We had to learn how to "fight" in a way that was not destructive. For me, it meant laying down my pride. For Lawrence, it meant laying down his anger. Neither was easy. I grew up a proud Texan from a proud, old Texan family. Lawrence had a lot of unresolved anger from his childhood. And while we were both saved and loved Yeshua and wanted to be like him, the sanctification process is a life-long one.

I sometimes think this is one of the reasons God brought Lawrence and I together. Iron sharpening iron ... Lawrence was a tool in God's hand, sanding out my rough edges, as I was tool in God's hand, softening out my husband's.

Everyone wants marriage bliss before they get married, right? And it is only right to work hard to attain it once you are married. But it doesn't come naturally. Marriage bliss is the product of hard work and a lot of reality checks.

Arguing over stupid, idiotic things that waste so much emotion and time is a threat to every marriage. What's more, little annoyances can become an open door to greater division. Don't let the enemy get a foothold because you are strong-willed and selfish.

In those early years I was too quick to be hurt over things that didn't really matter. I was offended.

Offense kills joy.

Offense kills trust.

Offense makes people walk on eggshells all the time around you and that is NO FUN!

FINDING A WAY TO GET BACK TO JOY TOGETHER, KEEPS YOU TOGETHER.

OLDER COUPLES WHO'D ALREADY FOUGHT THE GOOD FIGHT TAUGHT US HOW TO BUILD ONE ANOTHER UP, RATHER THAN TEAR ONE ANOTHER DOWN... WE LEARNED TO ONLY SPEAK WELL OF ONE ANOTHER. WE LEARNED TO LET ONE ANOTHER KNOW IF WE HAD HURT FEELINGS QUICKLY AND FORGIVE JUST AS FAST, RATHER THAN STUFFING OR HIDING OUR EMOTIONS OR HOLDING ON TO BITTERNESS AND "MAKING THE OTHER PAY."

PERHAPS THE MOST IMPORTANT LESSON WE LEARNED WAS TO KEEP OUR SENSE OF HUMOR. THE NUMBER ONE WAY TO GET THROUGH ROUGH DAYS, HOSPITAL STAYS, BUSINESS DEALS GONE SOUTH, ETC., *is to keep laughter near.*

You know what hurts the peace of your home faster than anything else? Refusing to admit you were wrong.

I WANT TO BE ABLE TO ADMIT WHEN I AM WRONG.

Did I just say that? Yes, I did.

I want to say sorry when my words do not bring life. You know, that moment when I choose the better way: When I "go low," instead of "go proud."

Going proud kills the peace faster than just about anything else. I have ruined a lot of chances to bring peace because of stubborn pride.

But... a quick turnaround, a repentant heart, a genuine "I'm sorry" met with a genuine "I forgive you" gets things back on track with your family and God.

There is one other factor that disturbs peace. And that factor is worry. Remember:

"Don't be pulled in different directions or worried about a thing. Be saturated in prayer throughout each day, offering your faith-filled requests before God with overflowing gratitude. Tell him every detail of your life, then God's wonderful PEACE that transcends human understanding, will make the answers known to you through Jesus Christ."

Philippians 4:6-7 (TPT)

The Peaceful Home

Is Fearless

Come Holy Spirit

The protection of peace starts within. When the house has been shaken by some terrible argument, misunderstanding, offense, a runaway negative-thought-train, or difficult situation, there is only one way to go, and that is towards God. The Father is always ready to touch your heart and comfort you, heal and bless you. Be still and let Him come. No rush. Just be still and let Him come. Just pray, "Come Holy Spirit."

Hard Times

Every life, no matter how blessed, experiences difficulty of some kind.

Family members who suffered divorce and spousal abuse.

Business ventures that never performed as we hoped.

Betrayed by people we trusted.

We've been stolen from and lied about.

We've suffered serious illness.

We've suffered.

WE ALL SUFFER.

But... that does not mean we are shaken.

And we boast in the hope of the glory of God. Not only so, but we also glory in our sufferings, because we know that suffering produces perseverance; perseverance, character; and character, hope. And hope does not put us to shame, because God's love has been poured out into our hearts through the Holy Spirit, who has been given to us.

~Romans 5:2-5

THE GREAT EXCHANGE

A FEW YEARS AGO, I FOUND MYSELF TRYING, ONCE AGAIN, NOT TO WAKE MY HUSBAND BY MY TOSSING AND TURNING. I HAD BEEN GRIPPED BY FEAR FOR THE MILLIONTH TIME OVER DIFFERENT THINGS. THIS WAS ANOTHER ONE OF THOSE NIGHTS, AND ON THIS NIGHT, I WAS PANICKED OVER THE SAFETY OF ONE OF MY CHILDREN. I HAD NO PEACE! AND SLEEP WAS THE LAST THING ON MY MIND.

AFTER ONE HOUR TURNED INTO TWO HOURS, AND TWO HOURS TO THREE, I STARTED TO CALL OUT TO THE LORD. INTERESTINGLY, I WASN'T PRAYING OVER MY CHILD. RATHER, I WAS PRAYING OVER MYSELF. FEAR HAD KEPT ME AWAKE SO MANY NIGHTS… AND ON THIS PARTICULAR NIGHT, SOMETHING JUST SNAPPED. I WAS DONE. I KNEW THAT MY FEAR WAS NOT GODLY. I NEEDED DELIVERANCE. I NEEDED A FRESH DOSE OF TRUST THAT GOD CARED ABOUT MY KIDS MORE THAN I DID. I DID NOT WANT TO SPEND ONE MORE SLEEPLESS NIGHT CONTROLLED BY FEAR AND ANXIETY.

MY PRAYER WENT SOMETHING LIKE THIS, "LORD, I CANNOT LIVE LIKE THIS ANYMORE! I DON'T WANT THIS FEAR TO CONTROL MY LIFE! I NEED YOUR TOUCH! I NEED YOUR HEALING IN MY LIFE. PLEASE, LORD! COME AND HEAL ME!"

TRUTH BE TOLD, I DON'T FULLY REMEMBER HOW THE REST OF THAT NIGHT WENT. I REMEMBER PRAYING A LOT. I REMEMBER TRYING TO GIVE THE LORD MY FEAR. AND THEN, I'M SURE I FELL INTO AN EXHAUSTED SLUMBER AND LIFE WENT ON.

BUT… A FEW MONTHS LATER, IT HIT ME. I HAD NOT BEEN AWAKENED AT 2 IN THE MORNING SINCE THAT NIGHT! MORE THAN THAT, I HAD RECEIVED A PHONE CALL THAT WOULD HAVE

IN THE PAST, SENT ME SPIRALING INTO FEAR. INSTEAD, I HAD RESPONDED IN TOTAL PEACE. THE LORD HAD HEARD MY CRY. HE HAD DELIVERED ME FROM FEAR. MORE THAN THAT, HE BEGAN TO SHOW ME HOW TRUSTWORTHY HE WAS WITH EVERY SITUATION THAT CAME MY WAY.

THERE ARE MANY THINGS YOU CAN DO TO HELP YOURSELF AVOID NEEDLESS WORRY AND ANXIETY. BUT, AT THE END OF THE DAY, THERE IS ONLY ONE PLACE YOU CAN GO TO RECEIVE PERFECT PEACE. JESUS HAS THE ABILITY AND THE DESIRE TO CALM THE STORMS IN YOUR LIFE. THE NEXT TIME YOU FIND YOURSELF AWAKE, HEARTBEAT FLUTTERING AWAY, PALMS SWEATY, AND YOUR THOUGHTS RACING, LET ME ENCOURAGE YOU TO GO TO THE ONE WHO HAS THE POWER TO SPEAK TO THE WAVES AND MOVE MOUNTAINS. WHAT'S MORE, HE HAS THE POWER TO DELIVER YOU FROM FEAR. BUT YOU HAVE TO GIVE IT TO HIM FIRST.

THAT IS THE GREAT EXCHANGE. YOU GIVE HIM FEAR, HE GIVES YOU CONFIDENCE. YOU GIVE HIM ANXIETY, HE GIVES YOU PEACE. YOU GIVE HIM ASHES, HE GIVES YOU BEAUTY.

THE GREAT EXCHANGE GIVES GOD PERMISSION TO GO TO PLACES IN YOUR LIFE THAT NEED NEW DIRECTION AND CORRECTION. IT GIVES GOD PERMISSION TO HEAL YOU AND SET YOU FREE. THE GREAT EXCHANGE HAS THE POWER TO CHANGE THE COURSE OF YOUR LIFE AND YOUR FAMILY.

GIVE GOD WHATEVER IT IS YOU NEED TO GIVE HIM IN ORDER TO RECEIVE HIS PEACE. HIS ABUNDANT, UNENDING, FAITHFUL PEACE. NO MATTER WHAT TROUBLE YOU MAY BE IN, HE IS THERE WITH YOU. HE IS ALWAYS THERE. HE IS ALWAYS FAITHFUL. HE IS ALWAYS TRUSTWORTHY.

If you aren't sure what you are holding on to that may be keeping you from receiving His peace, ask Him. He'll tell you! Some of the most basic "things" keeping us from receiving peace include:

Focusing on everything going wrong in the world

Fearing you will not be able to manage hardship

Spending free time escaping into media that is filled with lifeless messages

Getting stuck thinking there is no hope for the future

Not being able to believe that God is truly faithful

Not doing basic constructive things to build yourself up in courage and faith, like praying and worshiping and declaring out loud that God is good, especially when life is hard

Not taking time to meditate on Scripture and the presence of God

God promises us He will be with us in this life to give us His spirit and to guide us in the ways we should go. And even though He never promised it would be EASY, He did promise us His peace and presence... always!

AS PARENTS, WE DID NOT WANT TO HIDE REALITY FROM OUR CHILDREN. EVEN WHEN THEY WERE SMALL, WE TALKED THROUGH WHAT WAS HAPPENING (ON A CHILD-APPROPRIATE LEVEL). AS THEY GREW, THEY WERE PART OF MANY FAMILY DISCUSSIONS AND PRAYER MEETINGS, AS WE LAID OUR FEARS AT THE FEET OF JESUS AND WAITED FOR HIS GUIDANCE.

JOURNEYING TOGETHER THROUGH TRAUMA IS MUCH BETTER THAN TRAVELING ALONE. GOD GIVES US FAMILIES FOR A REASON.

EVEN WHEN THE GIRLS WERE QUITE YOUNG, LAWRENCE AND I CHOSE TO RESPECT THEIR VOICE AND OPINION. THEY MAY HAVE BEEN SMALL, BUT THEY HAD THE SAME HOLY SPIRIT! SOMETIMES LITTLE ONES ARE MORE ATTUNED TO THE SPIRITUAL ATMOSPHERE OF THE HOME THAN WE ARE.

ONE TIME, OUR SIX-YEAR-OLD JESS WAS HAVING SOME NIGHT FEARS. SHE DECIDED TO WRITE A LITTLE SONG TO HELP HER HEART HAVE COURAGE. IT WENT LIKE THIS:

Whenever I'm afraid,
I will trust in You.
Whenever I'm afraid,
I will trust in You,
Lord Jesus, I will trust in You,
Whenever I'm afraid,

Our family still sings this little song when
we are afraid and need courage.

You will be surprised what depth lies
beneath the heart of a little child, perhaps
they carry the word or song you need to
get through whatever valley you are being
asked to walk through.

THE RED SEA ROAD

Life goes so quickly, picking up speed with every passing year. Children grow up and leave home. High school . . . College . . . Graduate school . . . And then, it stops. Suddenly. Brazenly.

At times when the diagnosis looked frighteningly bad, when Lawrence was allowed to come home only to have to call an ambulance to take us back to the hospital yet again, God filled us with some sort of supernatural trust and peace. We were in a new zone. We were walking a new road of faith. God was doing something new through all this upheaval. We just didn't know what it was going to look like yet. The family call was changing. It was time to revise our mission statement and find out how God wanted us to respond.

From here on out, nothing would ever be the same. Not one thing. As many life-and-death situations do, our journey had forged a new boldness. The G5s (what we called our little tribe) had decided that life was more valuable and how we lived needed to change. Even though we had always been set on living for God, we wanted to go the distance and be willing to risk it all to go into the MYSTERIOUS BEYOND with the Lord.

There is a moment when you have a split second to choose which way you are going to go, especially when something traumatic is facing you. You have a choice which direction you are going to go in your mind, in your heart, in your emotions. You can literally "lose it." Or... you can trust God. I won't say I didn't lose it once or twice. Tears were shed. It took everything in me to trust. But we did choose to trust.

DAVE SEQUERIA, A BROTHER TO LAWRENCE AND ME AND AN UNCLE TO THE GIRLS, SHOWED UP FOR A VISIT. UNCLE DAVE, AS THE GIRLS CALL HIM, WAS WORKING ON SEVERAL PROJECTS REMODELING HOMES AND RENTING THEM OUT TO STUDENTS IN THE AREA. HE ASKED ME AS WE WERE THINKING ABOUT MOVING OUT OF THE HOME WE WERE IN, IF WE NEEDED TO GET RID OF ANY OF THE FURNITURE WE HAD. HE SAID HE COULD USE IT AND IF WE EVER WANTED IT BACK IT WOULD BE THERE FOR US.

I PAUSED, INWARDLY PRAYING, "LORD, I ALREADY GOT RID OF MULTIPLE ROOMS OF FURNITURE WHEN WE LEFT OUR LAST HOUSE... NOW YOU WANT ME TO GIVE DAVE THE REST OF IT?"

"IF YOU DON'T GET RID OF IT," I FELT THE LORD'S RESPONSE, "YOU WON'T BE ABLE TO SLIP THROUGH THE GATE TO THE NEXT SEASON."

"TAKE IT, DAVE," I ANSWERED, LOOKING AT LAWRENCE.

CLEARLY, THE LORD WAS WORKING TO MOVE US INTO A NEW WAY OF LIVING, A WAY MORE DEPENDENT ON HIM, MORE FREE, MORE FLEXIBLE AND MOVABLE, LESS WEIGHED DOWN, LITERALLY, BY STUFF. IN THE MOMENT, IT FELT LIKE THE ABSOLUTELY RIGHT DECISION. BUT THE NEXT DAY, WHEN DAVE SHOWED UP TO PICK UP THE FURNITURE, I STARTED TO WONDER IF I HAD MADE A MISTAKE.

CHAIRS, COUCHES, BOOKSHELVES, HUTCHES, TABLES, CHINA, CARPETS. THE LIST WENT ON AND ON. THE DINNER TABLE WAS THE BIG ONE. LAWRENCE AND I WERE CALLED TO HOSPITALITY! HOW COULD WE FULFILL OUR CALL WITHOUT OUR TABLE?

"GIVE, AND IT WILL BE GIVEN TO YOU. A GOOD MEASURE, PRESSED DOWN, SHAKEN TOGETHER AND RUNNING OVER, WILL BE POURED INTO YOUR LAP. FOR WITH THE MEASURE YOU USE, IT WILL BE MEASURED TO YOU." (LUKE 6:38) "WELL, LORD," I SAID AS I LET GO OF THE OLD SEASON AND WELCOMED THE NEW. "YOUR WAYS ARE NOT MY WAYS. IF YOU WANT MY TABLE, YOU CAN HAVE IT!"

IF THE LORD WANTED ME TO HOST, HE WOULD PROVIDE ME WITH EVERYTHING I NEEDED, FROM THE TABLE TO THE FOOD TO THE HOUSE!

AS DAVE DROVE AWAY, IT ALMOST FELT LIKE OUR FAMILY-CALLING WAS IN THE BACK OF IT, ALONG WITH THE TABLE AND THE OTHER "STUFF." BUT IT WASN'T. OH NO, NO CALLING IS DEPENDENT ON PHYSICAL CIRCUMSTANCES.

A WEEK OR SO LATER, WE PUT THE REST OF OUR THINGS (NOT MUCH) INTO A STORAGE UNIT AND MOVED INTO THE APTLY NAMED 'HOPE HOUSE,' A BEAUTIFUL MINISTRY HOME. IN THIS MOUNTAIN A-FRAME, THE G55 PAUSED FOR THE FIRST TIME IN A LONG TIME TO WAIT ON GOD FOR THE NEXT ASSIGNMENT.

THE TRUE SANCTUARY IS ACTUALLY A TRAVEL TRAILER IN YOUR HEART. YOU CAN HOOK IT UP AND IT MOVES WHEN YOU MOVE. YOU CAN HOST, LOVE, AND MINISTER TO PEOPLE ANYWHERE, AT ANY TIME. YOU CAN MAKE ANYONE FEEL AT HOME, EVEN IF YOU AREN'T "AT HOME."

LOOKING OVER THE MAGNIFICENT LASSEN VALLEY, LAWRENCE HAD THE MOST WONDERFUL IDEA. HE THOUGHT, "WELL, IF WE ARE RENTING A HOUSE HERE, WHY NOT RENT A HOME OVERSEAS FOR A FEW MONTHS?" (THAT IDEA WAS INSTANTLY GIVEN A UNANIMOUS "YES.")

AFTER WE PASSED THROUGH THE VALLEY OF THE SHADOW OF DEATH, LAWRENCE SAID IT WAS IN HIS HEART TO LIVE IN ISRAEL. WE HAD ALL WANTED TO LIVE IN ISRAEL SINCE WE VISITED FOR MADELINE'S BAT MITZVAH IN 2008. LAWRENCE FOUND US A HOME IN THE GALILEE. WE BOUGHT OUR TICKETS AND CAUGHT THE NEXT FLIGHT TO WHAT WOULD BECOME OUR TRUE "HOME AWAY FROM HOME."

It was here, on the shores of the lake where Jesus spent much of His ministry, that we tasted and saw that the Lord is good. It was here, under the shadows of Mount Tabor and Mount Arbel that we discovered the joy of the traveling sanctuary.

The mysterious beyond...

Leaving the comfort of our home of 22 years for a more nomadic life took a dose of courage. But we had almost lost Lawrence. The tests of life, individually and collectively, had taken a toll... But it had grown us up. As a family, we began to rely on each other more and more as we became increasingly transparent, honest, and whole.

You can help each member of your family embrace whatever the future may hold, no matter what you are facing. An illness. A new culture. An emotional challenge. Stay in the game. Stay close, even when it is the hardest thing you have ever done. The Lord helps us each step forward.

We each let go of agendas and timelines and gave in to the Holy Spirit and His mysterious plan. We called it the "mysterious beyond." He has your mysterious beyond in His perfect plan, and when we surrender to it, we are transformed.

Sometimes He brings you somewhere new to do something new...

Sometimes He makes you stay put to strengthen your roots. . .

The Open Door

AT HOME AND ABROAD, OUR DOOR IS OPEN.

WE NEVER KNOW WHO THE LORD WILL BRING THROUGH OUR DOOR, OR WHO WE WILL MEET WHEN WE WALK THROUGH THE DOOR TO THE OUTSIDE. WITH FRIENDSHIP, THE DOOR ALWAYS SWINGS BOTH WAYS. THE MORE WE WELCOME OTHERS, THE MORE WE ARE WELCOMED. THE MORE WE LOVE, THE MORE OF HIS LOVE WE FEEL. THE MORE WE COMFORT OTHERS, THE MORE WE ARE COMFORTED. IT DOESN'T EVEN MATTER IF YOU SPEAK THE SAME LANGUAGE. LOVE HAS A WAY OF SAYING MORE THAN WORDS CAN.

PEOPLE CAN TELL IF YOU LOVE THEM. PEOPLE CAN TELL IF YOU ARE A SAFE HAVEN. THAT PERSON IS LIKE A TREE PLANTED BY STREAMS OF WATER, WHICH YIELDS ITS FRUIT IN SEASON AND WHOSE LEAF DOES NOT WITHER. WHATEVER THEY DO PROSPERS.

Are You Ready to Build Your Sanctuary?

MAYBE IT IS TIME TO PRAY FOR LOVE TO BE BORN IN PLACES WHERE IT DOES NOT EXIST WITHIN YOU AND WITHIN YOUR HOME. GOD IS SO KIND. HE DOES WHAT YOU CANNOT DO BY YOURSELF. HE CAN CHANGE A DULL AND SELFISH HEART INTO ONE THAT IS OVERFLOWING WITH LIFE AND LOVE FOR OTHERS. TRUST ME. HE DID IT FOR ME! HIS LOVE IS FAITHFUL AND TRUE.

MAY THE LORD BLESS YOU WITH HIS NEVER ENDING LOVE AND GRACE TO BELIEVE IN MIRACLES FOR YOUR LIFE AND YOUR FAMILY.

I PRAY YOU WILL MAKE YOUR HOME, BOTH THE ONE YOU LIVE IN, AND THE ONE YOU ARE, INTO A SANCTUARY OF PEACE AND LOVE AND FREEDOM, A PLACE WHERE CREATIVITY IS WELCOMED AND MANY WILL FEEL ALIVE WITH THE BEAUTY THE LORD WILL SHOW THEM WITHIN ITS WALLS.

Lord Jesus,

Make me a living sanctuary, pure and holy, tried and true.

Make my home a safe space for Your Holy Spirit to move.

I give You the keys to my heart and home.

I welcome You at my table.

Teach me to be humble and to guard my gates.

Help me to fight the good fight in love.

Fill these walls with thanksgiving and praise until the day
we join You in the home You are preparing for us.

Our beautiful kids... above Zach and Madi Bowman,
Below, Zach Jess, Madi, and Emily

SEE WHAT THE GLASNERS ARE UP TO AT
WWW.HOPEHOUSEPRESS.CO

VISIT WWW.HOPEHOUSEPRESS.CO FOR MORE BOOKS THAT BUILD
FAMILIES, ENCOURAGE JOY, AND BRING LIFE.

TO PURCHASE PRINTS OF MADELINE'S ART INCLUDED IN THIS BOOK,
VISIT WWW.MADIBOWMAN.COM

Made in the USA
Middletown, DE
17 October 2022